GOOD QUESTIONS ON

BELIEF
&
DOUBT

{ A SIX-SESSION BIBLE STUDY }

Featuring **Christianity Today** Authors

Standard®
PUBLISHING

Cincinnati, Ohio

Published by Standard Publishing, Cincinnati, Ohio
www.standardpub.com

Also available: Good Questions on Heaven & Hell (ISBN 978-0-7847-2566-5); Good Questions on Right & Wrong (ISBN 978-0-7847-2567-2).

Printed in the United States of America

Project editor: Kelli B. Trujillo
Development editor: Laura Derico
Cover design: Faceout®Studio
Interior design: Dina Sorn at Ahaa! Design
Contributing study writers: Christopher Blumhofer, Joy-Elizabeth Lawrence, Jason & Alison Tarka, David & Kelli B. Trujillo, Kyle White, and Heather Gemmen Wilson

The "Good Questions" questions and articles that appear at the beginning of each chapter of Good Questions on Belief & Doubt are licensed from and copyright of Christianity Today International. Christianity Today magazine and its associated logos are trademarks of Christianity Today International, 465 Gundersen Drive, Carol Stream, Illinois 60188 (ChristianityToday.com).

ISBN 978-0-7847-2568-9

17 16 15 14 13 12 11   1 2 3 4 5 6 7 8 9

• CONTENTS •

WHAT'S IN THIS BOOK?

Everyone has questions. Some are easy: What can I wear today? Should I eat Fruity O's or Sugar Circles? Where did I put my keys? Some are heavy: What should I do with my life? Is this wrong or right? Where is God when I need him?

It's true that some people ask questions to distract, deceive, delay, or to stir up dissension. But good questions do something different. Good questions make us wonder, search, stretch, and grow.

With the Good Question Bible Studies series, we hope to help you cultivate an environment in which honest questions are welcomed, and the answers are sought together both through the consultation of respected research and through the experience of respectful—though no doubt often lively—conversation.

Each session begins with a question—a good question—which has been selected from some of those posed by readers and published in a feature section of *Christianity Today*. That question is followed by an article that was written in response by a well-known Christian author, experienced leader, and/or seasoned scholar.

But this is not where the study ends. **Launch** gives you a chance to open up the conversation with your group and build relationships through optional exercises. **Engage** allows the discussion to grow, building on the study of relevant Scripture passages. **Respond** and **React** ask you to reflect on the ideas you've talked about and think about what actions you might take. And finally, **Stretch** challenges each member to take the discussion beyond the group and into their relationships with others.

Throughout the studies **Delve Deeper** features provide an opportunity for more thought, while **For Further Study** lists point you in the direction of useful resources.

As every member uses these books, you will find that Good Question Bible Studies do not provide easy answers. But you will be met with an irresistible challenge: to wrestle with the issues and grow sharper, stronger, and closer to each other—and to God—along the way.

If your group enjoys these studies, don't miss the other titles in this series: *Good Questions on Heaven & Hell* (ISBN 978-0-7847-2566-5) and *Good Questions on Right & Wrong* (ISBN 978-0-7847-2567-2).

WHOSE TRUTH IS TRUE?
{ PROCLAIMING ONE TRUTH IN A POSTMODERN WORLD }

PREPARE

Before you meet with your small group, read this good question. Then read the response article written by Alister E. McGrath.

GQ 1 In a postmodern world in which people see many "truths" as equally valid, **how can you convince someone of the truth of salvation through Christ?**

One of the most obvious challenges Christians face from our postmodern culture is that there are so many "truths" that it seems impossible to speak of the one who described himself as the Truth. I have space to look at only two approaches to this question.

You could begin by affirming the importance of truth itself, and then move on to explain why the gospel indeed provides this truth. We all need to base our lives on something reliable, something that may be trusted. After all, who wants to base a life on delusions, lies, or dreams? The traditional evangelical emphasis upon the objectivity of truth affirms that we need to find something that is true in itself, not something that we would just like to be true.

You could then move on to affirming that the gospel is in-

deed true by focusing on the way in which it has transformed your own life. This allows you to build on two emphases that postmodernity finds particularly attractive—personal experience and telling stories.

> The gospel is not just true, it is real. Telling your personal story of faith is one of the best ways of declaring the transformative power of the gospel.

Our culture seems to have come to value stories over arguments. This allows you an opening to tell your story—the story of how the gospel became real in your life. The gospel is not just true, it is real. Telling your personal story of faith is one of the best ways of declaring the transformative power of the gospel.

You might like to try a second approach: Focusing on the attractiveness of the gospel. You could point out how Paul regarded all his achievements as being trivial compared with the unsurpassable richness of knowing Christ (Philippians 3:7, 8): "Whatever was to my profit I now consider loss for the sake of Christ. What is more, I consider everything a loss compared to the surpassing greatness of knowing Christ Jesus my Lord." These words resonate with the excitement of discovery and fulfillment. Paul had found something that ended his long quest for truth and meaning.

Jesus made a similar point in one of his parables. He compared the kingdom of heaven to a pearl of great price. "The kingdom of heaven is like a merchant looking for fine pearls. When he found one of great value, he went away and sold everything he had and bought it" (Matthew 13:45, 46). The merchant finds a priceless pearl for sale and decides that he will sell everything in order to possess it. Why? Because here is something of supreme value. Here is something worth pos-

sessing. Everything else he possesses seems of little value in comparison.

What the merchant had obtained previously was a preparation for this final purchase. When he saw the pearl, he knew that everything already in his possession seemed dull and lackluster in comparison.

Just as the brilliance of the sun drowns that of the stars, so that they can only be seen at night, so this great pearl led the merchant to see his own possessions as less than dazzling. What he had thought would satisfy him proved only to disclose his dissatisfaction and make him long for something that was beyond his grasp. When he saw that pearl, he knew he had to have it.

> The New Testament. . . . reassures us that truth and relevance are intrinsic to the gospel, part of its very fabric.

Thus you could make the point that the gospel is deeply satisfying, with the power to change human lives. And this is no delusion, no human invention to ease the pain of life. It is grounded in the bedrock of truth. The New Testament offers us hints as to how we can proclaim the gospel in a variety of contexts. But above all, it reassures us that truth and relevance are intrinsic to the gospel, part of its very fabric.

Yes, we face new challenges. But we can trust that the gospel is able to meet those challenges, and that we too can rise to them.

Alister E. McGrath is Professor of Theology, Ministry and Education, and Head of the Center for Theology, Religion, and Culture at King's College, London. "The Real Gospel" was first published in the December 2002 issue of Christianity Today.

LAUNCH

OPTIONAL EXERCISE

Your group may want to begin your meeting with this activity. You'll need **blank paper, black pens or markers,** and **tape.**

What do people in our culture think about religion, about God, or about truth? Grab some paper (yes, even those of you who are not artistically inclined) and sketch a simple cartoon person with a speech bubble to represent a particular familiar viewpoint or opinion about these issues. You can draw a rudimentary stick-figure or a full-blown cartoon—whatever style you'd like. In the speech bubble, craft a short statement that sums up the character's perspective on religion, God, or truth.

For example, you might draw a stick figure (perhaps in a yoga pose) representing New Age pop spirituality—her speech bubble could read: "You may call him 'God' but that's just your label for your higher consciousness." Or how about a sketch of a world-traveling hipster with a speech bubble that reads: "Don't be a hater! I value and appreciate all the world's religions."

As a group, try to create cartoons representing a wide diversity of viewpoints you observe in our culture. If you need ideas, consider sketching one of the following characters:

- a nominal, noncommitted Christian
- a modern-day hedonist
- an adherent of Islam
- a financially successful person
- a Buddhist
- a materialist who believes only in science and reason
- a formerly-religious person turned atheist

As you finish your cartoons, tape them onto a wall in your

meeting area to create a "crowd" of various worldviews within our postmodern culture.

Together, look at what you've created to see if any major worldviews or philosophies are missing; briefly talk about any important perspectives that have been overlooked.

As you discuss the questions in today's study, keep the "crowd" in mind. Reference their viewpoints as you consider how to affirm God's truth in a world jam-packed with so many other "truths."

In an essay published with his album *18*, musical artist Moby reflected on his views about religion and truth, writing. "Our simple, human level is so tiny compared to the vastness of the universe, that we should never think that our personal beliefs are universal or objectively true."[1]

1 You probably have friends and loved ones who think just like Moby. What makes a postmodern worldview like this attractive? Why do you think people hold to this view of the world?

2 What are some of the personal and social implications of holding a subjective view of truth?

ENGAGE

THERE ARE MANY PERCEIVED TRUTHS IN THE WORLD

It is widely recognized that we're moving toward a post-Christian culture in which the Christian narrative is not only rejected, but it's viewed as completely irrelevant. The Bible can no longer be assumed as a common starting point or even a reference point for ideas or values.

Philosophers and culturists attribute many reasons for the rise of postmodernism and post-Christianity. In addition to the cultural impact of thinkers such as Darwin, Nietzsche, and Freud that marked the early twentieth century, today we see two especially significant factors. First, the information boom of the twentieth century contributed to a pervasive sense of doubt in our ability to know objective truth. And second, globalization has created a greater awareness and appreciation of the many different worldviews.[2]

Huston Smith, a secular world religions scholar, claims that we have three possible responses to all the religious and worldview options surrounding us. We could either hold a single religious belief as superior to the others; we could believe that all religions speak the same essential truths and are "basically alike"; or as he prefers, we could recognize the differences of all the world's religious beliefs yet value what they offer collectively as a composite picture—the same way the various sections of a stained-glass window "divide the light of the sun into different colors.[3]

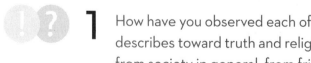

1   How have you observed each of the three stances Huston describes toward truth and religion? Draw upon examples from society in general, from friends or people you know, and from popular entertainment.

Writing during the initial rise of Darwinian and Nietzchean thought, Christian thinker and humorist G. K. Chesterton appears to have anticipated our current culture when he wrote, "[W]hat we suffer from today is humility in the wrong place. Modesty has moved from the organ of ambition. Modesty has settled upon the organ of conviction; where it was never meant to be. A man was meant to be doubtful about himself, but undoubting about the truth; this has been exactly reversed."[4]

Chesterton went on to claim that if the culture did in fact depart from the idea of God, it would necessarily leave behind the world of objectivity. He wrote, "In so far as religion is gone, reason is going. . . . [I]n the act of destroying the idea of Divine authority we have largely destroyed the idea of human authority by which we do a long division sum."[5] In other words, Chesterton jokingly posits, we're headed down a path of doubting truth so much that eventually we'll even doubt our ability to do math!

> **DELVE DEEPER**
>
> If you'd like, explore this question as a group or on your own:
>
> Though it can at times seem overwhelming to consider all the apparent options for belief in our world, Christian scholar James W. Sire offers us a sense of perspective. In *The Universe Next Door*, he writes, "Worldviews . . . are not infinite in number. In a pluralistic society they seem to exist in profusion, but the basic issues and options are actually rather small."[6] He claims that there are at most ten main worldviews, including theism, naturalism, pantheistic monism, and postmodernism.[7]
>
> How can this perspective help you open a dialogue with those who hold a more subjective, postmodern view?

2 What's your response to Chesterton's observations about modesty and conviction? About God and human reason? Explain?

Near the beginning of his epistle to the Romans, Paul made some strong claims about humanity's interaction with *aletheia*, translated as "truth" (1:18, 25). Read the context of Paul's assertions in Romans 1:18-25. (You can also glance at 2:2, 8, 20 for additional insights into his use of the word *truth*).

3 In light of the context of the broader passage, how would you sum up Paul's definition of the words *suppress*, *truth*, and *wickedness* in Romans 1:18? What does he mean by each of these terms?

4 In what ways do the ideas in this passage connect with our current conversation about truth and culture?

JESUS CLAIMS HE IS ULTIMATE TRUTH

One of the most intriguing conversations in history took place between Jesus and Pilate, recorded for us near the end of John's Gospel (John 18:33-38). The climactic point in the conversation came when Jesus stated, "I came into the world, to testify to the truth. Everyone on the side of truth listens to me" (v. 37). Pilate abruptly closed the conversation by saying, "What is truth?" (v. 38).

Commenting on this passage, Christian theologian Anthony C. Thiselton suggests, "The truth is shown to be a reality, based on

God's revelation. . . . Pilate remains baffled because there are certain questions about truth which can be answered only when a man is fully open to hear the witness of Jesus."[8]

Read **John 18:33-38** in light of Thiselton's comments.

5 How do you interpret Pilate's response to Jesus? Do you agree with Thiselton's reading of the text? Why or why not?

6 What do you understand Jesus to be saying about his kingship and the nature of truth? Explain.

7 How do Jesus' comments here align with Paul's words in Romans 1:18-25? Describe how you see these two passages interacting.

In John, Jesus also taught that truth sets us free from the slavery of sin (8:32). Truth ultimately gives us a sense of fulfillment as our hope is rightly placed in our creator, Savior, and sanctifier—our God. Jesus made clear that knowing and experiencing this truth naturally requires a response of faithful obedience. He spoke about this idea in his conversation with Nicodemus (3:21) and with the woman at the well (4:23, 24). And, most importantly, he declared, "I am the way and the truth and the life" (14:6). In John we see that truth is not only exclusive to Christ, but it has been revealed by God, it is contrasted with our world, and it's effective to change lives.

 8 Review these key passages about truth in John: **3:20, 21; 4:23, 24; 8:31, 32; and 14:6**. How do Jesus' teachings here recast the way we are to present truth to our postmodern, post-Christian world? How can we make the truth of the gospel more palpable and observable?

WE SHOULD ENGAGE TRUTH WITH CONFIDENCE AND HUMILITY

It's not difficult to see why a postmodern person would view Christians as either ignorant or arrogant. After all, how can someone claim to make sense of all that "stuff" out there? To know *the* answer to the mysteries of the existence? In our culture, the mere claim that there is objective, absolute truth seems presumptuous.

It's not just the claim of truth that makes Christians seem arrogant, but the way some Christians approach the whole conversation can put people off. In seeking to defend the truth, Christians may respond to seekers' difficult questions with quick, logical, packaged solutions rather than by truly engaging with the complexity of the issues and the emotions involved. For example, a Christian might reply to the question, "If there is a loving and all-powerful God, why does he allow so much evil and suffering in the world?" with a well-reasoned theodicy—and an absolute lack of empathy and humility. Though the answer may be "right," the Christian's failure to acknowledge the very real difficulties of the issue can come across as condescending and make the Christian's answer seem trivial and inadequate.

9 How can Christians practically defend truth while remaining open to dialogue on difficult issues? How might the claim of truth invite rather than suppress dialogue?

There are many issues that require a humble response even within Christian faith. As finite beings that exist in a supernatural world, there are some scriptural truths that are too difficult for us to fully comprehend.

The Bible affirms the reality that there are mysteries beyond our grasp. Read and consider the declaration about God in **Deuteronomy 29:29**, Paul's remarks about love and spiritual gifts in **1 Corinthians 13:12**, and the "hymn of wisdom" in **Job 28:23-28** which concludes that God (not humankind) is the sole possessor of wisdom.

How can we respond to difficult questions or unclear truths? Rather

DELVE DEEPER

If you'd like, explore these questions as a group or on your own:

In his article Alister McGrath offers two suggestions when it comes to sharing our faith in a postmodern world. First, we ought to "affirm the importance of truth." But, McGrath goes on to suggest an approach that sometimes receives less attention; beyond only asserting truth in our postmodern culture, he suggests that we should also focus on "the attractiveness of the gospel." After all, McGrath reminds us, the truth of Jesus is "deeply satisfying, with the power to change human lives."

Consider the motifs of hunger and thirst, ultimate satisfaction, and true life that Jesus uses in John 4:7-14 and 6:32-35, 47-51.

How are these descriptions of the truth of the good news relevant to our world today? To your non-Christian friends or loved ones? How could a more accurate presentation of the gospel (which includes these ideas of satisfaction and life) make the truth more attractive to our contemporary audience?

than being embarrassed or troubled by mysteries within Christian doctrine, we can embrace them as we ask questions and continue to seek out answers. The church ought to be a place that invites and facilitates engagement with difficult ideas. Believers and seekers alike ought to find their questions and concerns validated. And, these questions ought to be met with reasonable, humble, and thoughtful responses.

 10 What would be the cultural impact of a truth-proclaiming Christian community that authentically embraces mystery and values difficult questions?

RESPOND

Think of someone you know who holds a subjective, postmodern view of truth. In light of your group's discussion, what would you most like that person to know about Christianity? Why?

REACT

Considering all you've studied and discussed, how have you been personally challenged or inspired by this exploration of truth? Briefly write some of your concluding thoughts in the space provided.

Wrap up your time by praying together as a group. Focus specifically on your desire to be a powerful witness to truth in our postmodern and increasingly post-Christian world.

STRETCH

Set aside time on your own soon after your small group meeting for prayerful contemplation.

Find a space where you can be quiet and alone; if you'd like, bring along paper and a pen.

Mathematician and Christian philosopher Blaise Pascal once wrote this about mystery and truth: "If we submit everything to reason our religion will be left with nothing mysterious or supernatural. If we offend the principles of reason our religion will be absurd and ridiculous."[9]

FOR FURTHER STUDY
BOOKS

- *Are All Religions One?* by Douglas Groothius (InterVarsity Press)
- *The Faith* by Charles Colson and Harold Fickett (Zondervan)
- *How Postmodernism Serves (My) Faith* by Crystal L. Downing (InterVarsity Press)
- *Orthodoxy* by G. K. Chesterton (Ignatius)
- *The Passionate Intellect* by Alister McGrath (InterVarsity Press)
- *A Primer on Postmodernism* by Stanley J. Grenz (Eerdmans)
- *Truth or Consequences* by Millard J. Erickson (InterVarsity Press)
- *unChristian* by David Kinnaman (Baker Books)
- *The Universe Next Door* by James W. Sire (InterVarsity Press)

ONLINE RESOURCES

- "God Is Not Dead Yet" by William L. Craig, from *Christianity Today* (www.christianitytoday.com/ct/2008/july/13.22.html)
- "The Postmodern Crackup" by Charles Colson, from *Christianity Today* (www.christianitytoday.com/ct/2003/december/24.72.html)
- "Richard Dawkins and Alister McGrath"— Alister McGrath interviewed by well-known atheist Richard Dawkins (video.google.com/videoplay?docid=6474278760369344626#)
- "This Samaritan Life: How to Live in a Culture that is Vaguely Suspicious of the Church" by Tim Stafford, from *Christianity Today* (www.christianitytoday.com/ct/2008/february/21.47.html)

For Pascal, both supernatural mystery and reasoned, straight-forward truths were essential aspects of his Christian faith. What about you? What supernatural, incomprehensible aspects of God or mysteries of Christian doctrine are important to you? And what key, straightforward biblical truths are central to who you are and what you believe?

Create a mental (or actual) list of the mysterious truths and comprehensible truths that you hold dear. Focus on them, one by one, thanking God for them and embracing their place in your faith.

Study written by David and Kelli B. Trujillo. David is a Bible teacher and Kelli is an author and editor (www.kellitrujillo.com). They are columnists for *GROUP* magazine and serve together as adult ministry leaders in their church in Indianapolis.

WHY DID GOD CREATE PEOPLE WHO REJECT HIM?
{ CREATOR'S DILEMMA }

Before you meet with your small group, read this good question.
Then read the response article written by Timothy George.

GQ 2 Why did an omniscient God create humankind knowing
that people, in every generation, would reject him?

*The honest answer to this question is, we don't know—at
least not in a cocksure, foolproof way that takes the risk out
of faith and the mystery out of revelation. The Bible says
that "the secret things belong to the LORD our God" (Deuteronomy 29:29). And yet this is a natural and reasonable
question to ask. We can say four things in response:*

*First, everything God does, by either explicit decree or per-
mission, has an ultimate beneficial purpose. This includes the
fact of hell and God's judgment against rebellious sinners, as
well as the blessings of heaven and salvation in Christ. Love
and holiness are both essential attributes of God, and they
are not in competition with one another. As with Job, in the
face of suffering and mystery we are tempted to accuse God
of wrongdoing and put him in the dock. But God's answer to*

Job reaches us as well: "Would you condemn me to justify yourself?" (Job 40:8).

Second, this question assumes that human beings are victims caught in the vise of an inexorable fate. But the Bible teaches that God in his goodness has created a world of moral order, one in which men and women are free moral agents. By creating Adam and Eve in his image and likeness, God gave them a quality of relationship with him that no other creature has. God's creative act was so great that he trusted them with freedom. Unfortunately, freedom includes the freedom to turn away from God, and that is what Adam and Eve did. The fact that God knew beforehand what they would do in no way abrogated their capacity to act and do as they chose. God condemns no one unjustly. God is the judge of all the earth, and he will do right by everyone. On the final day of judgment, no one will be able to stand before God and say to him, "I have been treated unfairly by you!"

> By creating Adam and Eve in his image and likeness, God gave them a quality of relationship with him that no other creature has. . . . he trusted them with freedom.

Of course, exactly how the inequities of this life will be seen in the tapestry of eternity remains imponderable. But we do know that God's plan is free and purposive, that he does not compel or coerce human creatures made in his image, and that nothing can ultimately thwart his glory and grace.

Third, it may seem that we can get God off the hook by denying his absolute foreknowledge of future events, by seeing Creation as an open-ended experiment about which even God is in the dark. Rather than taking the problem of evil seriously, though, such a view of God trivializes it. We would not praise a doctor who produced horrible deformities while experimenting with human cloning.

Nor can we find solace in a disabled deity whose creative power unleashes a floodtide of suffering and evil over which he has no certain knowledge and only limited control. Such a god might deserve to be pitied—but not worshipped and adored. This is why orthodox Christians of all confessions have affirmed God's complete foreknowledge of the future, however much they may have differed on issues such as election and predestination.

Finally, Jesus Christ is the surest window into the heart of God. When Martin Luther was asked difficult questions such as the one posed here, he replied by encouraging his troubled friends to "look to the wounds of Jesus." That same advice had been given to him as a young man, when, plagued by guilt, he doubted whether he could ever be accepted by a holy God. By focusing on Christ, he discovered the doctrine of justification by faith alone. In Jesus Christ, God's grace and truth were realized in perfect equipoise. In Jesus we see that God is unspeakably generous, "abundant in goodness and truth" (Exodus 34:6, KJV), and at the same time a God of uncompromised purity and righteousness. In Jesus Christ the Creator has become our Redeemer, the Judge has received our judgment. Through his death and resurrection, the way to eternal life has been forever opened to all who turn from selfishness and sin and in simple trust commit themselves to Christ for all time and eternity.

Timothy George, a Christianity Today *executive editor, is dean of Beeson Divinity School at Samford University in Birmingham. "Has God Played Fair?" was first published in the November 2001 issue of* Christianity Today.

LAUNCH

OPTIONAL EXERCISE

Your group may want to begin with this activity. Set up the board game Scrabble and divide your group into four equal-sized teams. Team 1 should play by the normal Scrabble rules; the remaining three teams should each play by a new, unique "rule" that you won't find in the game instructions. Here are suggestions, but you can also make up your own rule modifications:

1. Team 1 plays by the normal rules found in the game's instructions.
2. Team 2 can only play with five letter tiles at a time.
3. Team 3 can always peek at the letter tiles they draw before selecting them.
4. Team 4 always gets a double turn.

(Or, if you'd like, play a different board game and add similar inequity and unfairness to the rules of play.)

Obviously, this game is meant to be unfair! Play for a few quick rounds and see how things turn out, then talk about the following questions:

- How did it feel to be on your team? (At least one member of each team should answer.)
- Did you find yourself competing and trying to win even though you knew the game wasn't fair? Explain.
- Was it fun to play a game that was fundamentally unfair? Why or why not?

From an early age, we're hardwired to sniff out any hint of unfairness in a given situation. When kids complain of unfairness, often parents and teachers respond by playing the "life isn't fair" card.

1 Share about a time when you were growing up and you felt you were treated unfairly. What happened? Did somebody give you the "life isn't fair" line?

Even though we know life isn't exactly "fair," it can still be a bitter pill to swallow, especially when we see injustices in the world.

2 How fair do you expect life to be? How fair do you expect God to be? Explain. Talk about how you evaluate fairness.

Many people—both Christians and non-Christians—struggle to understand how the biblical teachings about God's omniscience, God's love, and unbelievers' eternal destiny in Hell can all fit together. On the surface, it can seem like huge injustices exist in God's plan for human beings. The following discussion will explore the complex issues of fairness and free will.

ENGAGE

GOD CREATES US WITH FREEDOM OF CHOICE

As Timothy George explains, God lovingly created humans to be "free moral agents." Adam and Eve began their existences in a perfect, one-hundred-percent-right relationship with God. But as free moral agents, Adam and Eve had the God-given ability to choose to sin or not sin.[1]

Briefly review **Genesis 2:4-25** on your own, then read **3:1-24** out loud as a group.

1
Adam and Eve were created with the freedom to choose to eat from the tree of the knowledge of good and evil (2:15-17). Do you think it was unfair for God to put them in this position? or was it loving to give them a choice? Explore the rationale behind both points of view.

Think about both the immediate consequences Adam and Eve experienced (3:21-24) as well as the implications for future generations (2:17; 3:14-19).

2
How do you view God's response to their sinful choice? Was it fair and justified?

3
In his article George asserts that everything God does has an "ultimate beneficial purpose." What do you think of this statement in light of Adam and Eve's sin and the fall of humankind? Explain.

GOD'S WAYS ARE MYSTERIOUS, BUT WE CAN TRUST HIM

As much as we would like to believe that God is completely comprehensible, we must admit and confess that God's ways are not our ways. God is holy and omniscient—he operates on a completely different level than we do. At times, this reality can feel unsettling.

Take a moment to read and quietly think about this quotation from Karl Barth: "Just because He is this free and loving God, He is not interchangeable with any creature in heaven or on earth, or with the likeness of any product of human imagination. He is sovereign, and His name is holy above every other name, and not to be named with any other in the same breath."[2]

In our modern-day emphasis on having a "friendship" or "relationship" with Jesus (which is, of course, a very good thing!), it can become all too easy to begin to casually relate to God—to lose sight of how amazing, holy, and "set apart" God really is from us.

> ## DELVE DEEPER
>
> If you'd like, explore this question as a group or on your own:
>
> Many followers of Christ have very different views about God's sovereignty and our free will. Essentially, the debate comes down to whether people are completely free and able to accept Jesus' salvation or if God predestines those who will be saved. What do you think?
>
> As a group, compare and contrast the following passages that may seem contradictory on the issue of predestination: John 6:44, 65; Romans 9; 1 Timothy 2:3-6; Titus 2:11; and 2 Peter 3:9. Try to keep your discussion candid, friendly, and affirming as you talk about this complex topic.

4 What do we miss out on when we overemphasize the idea of friendship with God and, as a result, underestimate his awesome, mysterious "otherness"? How might this imbalance affect one's worship, one's theology, or even one's evangelism?

In light of the difficult question of why God would create people who would reject him, read **Isaiah 40:12-31** as a group. Notice how Isaiah focuses both on God's greatness and sovereignty over creation as well as his intimate knowledge of and care for the created. The same God that separated the sky and seas holds the depths of the oceans in his hand and also calls every star by name.

 5 Does God's infinite greatness draw out feelings of fear or comfort in you? or both? Explain.

 6 Share about a time when you felt like you had no control over a situation and you had to trust in God's sovereignty. What feelings and questions did you have to wrestle with?

WE CAN FIND THE ULTIMATE ANSWER IN JESUS' LOVE

While God is holy and sovereign, he passionately loves his creation and desires everyone to know him. After the fall of humankind, over and over again in Scripture we see God reaching out to his lost creation in order that they could know him and worship him.

In Jesus, God performed the ultimate act of love toward the world by sending his Son as a sacrifice; the creator died for the created and the judge became the judgment. Thus, we can echo George's statement: "Jesus Christ is the surest window into the heart of God." While this may not directly answer the question of why God would create those he knows will reject him, it does point us toward the ultimate truth that God loves us and wants everyone to know his grace and mercy.

Read the following passages together in this order: **Romans 1:18-32; Ephesians 2:1-3; Romans 5:6-11; Ephesians 2:4-10.**

7 How does Paul describe God's love for the world despite its fallen state? Sum up Paul's main ideas in your own words.

8 Christians have a reputation for looking down on the world with an attitude of disdain and judgment. Is this a well-earned stereotype or an unfair assessment? How does this contrast with how God views and relates to the "lost" in our world?

George appropriately ends his article by focusing on the Son of God: "In Jesus Christ, God's grace and truth were realized in perfect equipoise. In Jesus we see that God is unspeakably generous, 'abundant in goodness and truth' (Exodus 34:6, *KJV*), and at the same time a God of uncompromised purity and righteousness."

9 How do you think God's generosity and his "uncompromised purity and righteousness" work together?

Jesus is creator, Savior, judge, and our only hope for redemption and relationship with God. As one theologian described Jesus' profound and powerful love, "God is not greater than he is in this humiliation [on the cross]. God is not more glorious than he is in this self-surrender. God is not more powerful than he is in this helplessness. . . . Here he himself is love with all his being."[3] If you want to know about God, then you must first start at the cross. The cross is God's yes to the world; his offer of reconciliation and love. Ultimately, Jesus Christ is God's agent of salvation and hope for his creation.

10 How can the cross indirectly answer the big question about God creating those who'd reject him? Is it a sufficient answer? Why or why not?

RESPOND

The question of how a loving God could create people he foreknew would go to Hell isn't just a challenge for agnostics or spiritual seekers—it can be a tough one for Christians to wrestle with too! Based on your discussion, what point or idea best helps you personally grapple with this question? Talk through your ideas together.

REACT

Pondering perplexing and amazing truths about God—his sovereignty, his power, his omniscience—should draw us into awe, into worship. Take a moment now to write words or phrases expressing your response to these amazing truths about who God is.

As a group, have each person mention two to three people they know who are not followers of Jesus. Spend time praying for each person by name, asking God to draw those people to him. Also ask God to create opportunities for you to share about God's love and what Jesus has done for them.

STRETCH

Set aside time on your own soon after your small group meeting for a time of personal reflection and creative writing.

Got a favorite song? Many of us love music because we can really relate to certain songs. They powerfully capture and convey honest,

FOR FURTHER STUDY
BOOKS

- *Chosen but Free* by Norman L. Geisler (Bethany House)
- *Debating Calvinism: Five Points, Two Views* by Dave Hunt and James White (Multnomah)
- *Evangelism and the Sovereignty of God* by J. I. Packer (InterVarsity Press)
- *Four Views on Hell* by William Crockett and Stanley N. Grundy, eds. (Zondervan)
- *Good Questions on Heaven & Hell* (Standard Publishing)
- *Let the Nations be Glad!* by John Piper (Baker Academic)
- *Predestination and Free Will* by David Basinger and Randall Basinger, eds. (InterVarsity Press Academic)

ONLINE ARTICLES

- "The Craig-Bradley Debate: Can a Loving God Send People to Hell?" transcript from Christian apologist William Lane Craig (www.leaderu.com/offices/billcraig/docs/craig-bradley1.html)
- "Don't Hate Me Because I'm Arminian" by Roger E. Olson, from *Christianity Today* (www.christianitytoday.com/ct/1999/september6/9ta087.html)
- "Three Models of Hell" by R. Todd Mangum, from *Christianity Today* (www.christianitytoday.com/ct/2007/february/38.118.html)

raw emotion. This study grapples with some difficult questions and may have stirred up conflicting feelings within you as you've wrestled through how God's sovereignty, love, and justice all work together.

Scripture is filled with songs, poems, and prayers that commemorate deliverance, a victory, protection, and so on. But these songs also capture the essence of the writers' feelings—the raw reality of the human experience. Consider reading through these biblical songs and poems:

- Moses' reflection on God's deliverance of his people (Exodus 15:1-21).
- David's poetic praise about the construction of God's Temple (1 Chronicles 29:10-13).
- One of David's songs about God's power and sovereignty (Psalm 103).
- Mary's poem-song about her miraculous pregnancy (Luke 1:46-55).

Now grab some paper and a pencil and spend some time crafting your own song lyrics, poem, or prayer focusing on God's power, sovereignty, and wisdom. (If you'd like, draw upon the words and phrases you jotted down during the React portion of the study.) Focus on the idea that, though we may not always understand God's ways, we can rest assured that he knows the beginning and the end, has a purpose for everything, and is in control. In your writing, aim to honestly express your thoughts, ideas, and emotions—and don't feel any pressure to create a musical or literary masterpiece! Remember that what you write is just between you and God, so simply aim to be authentic.

When you're done writing your first draft, read it aloud.

Study written by Jason and Alison Tarka. Jason and Alison live in Portland, Oregon, where Jason leads worship, teaches theology, and writes for small groups. Alison is a stay-at-home mother, violinist, blogger, and freelance writer.

HOW COULD THE ETERNAL GOD DIE?

{ DIVINE IMMORTALITY AND THE DEATH OF CHRIST }

PREPARE

Before you meet with your small group, read this good question. Then read the response article written by J. I. Packer.

GQ 3 Since Jesus was divine, how do we explain his death? **Can the eternal God die?**

The background to this question is today's post-Christian perplexity as to whether physical death is the end of the person who lived in (or, more accurately, through) the now-defunct body.

All brands of materialists—scientific, philosophical, theoretical Marxist, secular irreligious, and antireligious European and American—say it is. Everyone else, from ancient Egyptians, Greeks, and Norsemen to every form of religion and tribal culture the world has ever seen, has always been sure it isn't. Historic, Bible-based Christianity is part of this consensus. On the nature of postmortem life there are great differences, but on its reality, agreement has been so widespread that current Western skepticism about survival seems a mere local oddity.

So the first thing to say is that all human selves, with all the powers of remembering, relating, learning, purposing, and enjoying that make us who we are, survive death, and by dying are actually set free from all shrinkings of personal life due to physical factors—handicaps, injuries, and deteriorations of body and mind; torture and starvation; Alzheimer's disease, Down syndrome, AIDS, and the like. This was true for both Jesus and the believing criminal to whom he said, as crucifixion drained their lives away, "Today you will be with me in paradise"; and it will be just as true for you and me.

To be sure, the ugliness and pain and aftermath of dying as we know it is the penalty of sin. For anyone unconverted in heart, who is thus already "dead in transgressions" (Ephesians 2:5), dying means entering more deeply into the death state (meaning, separation from that sharing with God that Scripture calls "life"). We need to be clear that as our penal substitute, Jesus "tasted death" (Hebrews 2:9) in this deep sense precisely to ensure that we would never have to taste it. The natural view of his cry from the cross, "My God, my God, why have you forsaken me?" (first words of Psalm 22, Matthew 27:46), is that he was telling the bystanders, and through them the world, that in fulfillment of prophecy he was already undergoing deep death, as we may call it, during those dark hours. Godforsakenness was the hell into which Jesus entered on the cross; as Rabbi Duncan once told a class, with tears in his eyes, "it was damnation, and he took it lovingly."

Incarnation gave the eternal Son of God capacity for this experience. "The Word became flesh" in the sense that without ceasing to be anything that he was before, he added to himself all that humanness in this world involves—namely, life through

> Jesus "tasted death" in this deep sense precisely to ensure that we would never have to taste it.

a body bounded by space and time, with all the glories, limitations, and vulnerabilities that belong to our everyday existence, including in due course leaving behind the body through which one has consciously lived all along. Shakespeare, we know, acted in the plays he authored and produced, and that is a faint parallel to the co-Creator living an ordered creaturely life within his own created world.

> The certain fact is that as his life was a divine person's totally human life, so his dying was a divine person's totally human death.

There are mysteries here beyond our grasp—how, for instance, the sense of human and of divine identity meshed; how the Son controlled his divine powers so as not to overstep the limits of human finiteness; how entire dependence on his Father's leading for every word and deed made him the most unnerving initiative taker ever seen; and so on. But the certain fact is that as his life was a divine person's totally human life, so his dying was a divine person's totally human death.

Nor was Jesus' dying the end of the story. His rising from the dead, of which Scripture speaks as the work of all three persons of the Trinity (John 10:17, 18; Acts 13:30; 1 Peter 3:18), was a fresh exercise of the power that made the world and effected the Incarnation, leading on to the further work of power whereby the Son was glorified and enthroned, now to live as the God-Man in unbroken fellowship with his Father forever (Romans 6:9, 10). His resurrection and glorification is the prototype of what awaits all believers, and his experience of dying guarantees that when it is time for us to leave this world his loving, supportive, sympathizing presence with us will, as William Williams's hymn puts it, "land me safe on Canaan's side." Such is God's great grace.

Theology is not for casual curiosity, but for heartfelt doxology, and never more so than when Christ's death is the theme. So Williams's contemporary Charles Wesley was really giving our question a perfect and final answer when he wrote:

> *Tis mystery all! The Immortal dies:*
> *Who can explore his strange design?*
> *In vain the first-born seraph tries*
> *To sound the depths of love divine.*
> *Tis mercy all! Let earth adore,*
> *Let angel minds inquire no more.*

J. I. Packer is Board of Governors' Professor of Theology at Regent College and a member of the editorial council for Christianity Today. "Did God Die on the Cross?" was first published in the April 1999 issue of Christianity Today.

LAUNCH

OPTIONAL EXERCISE

Your group may want to begin your meeting with this activity. You'll need at least **one computer with Internet access.**

Is Elvis really dead? Some people think he's still alive—along with Michael Jackson, rapper Tupac Shakur, and Princess Di. Perhaps you know of other celebrities who have supposedly been sighted after their publicized deaths. Together, search the Internet to find reasons why these individuals are still considered to be alive. (Hint: "Elvis lives" will bring up a lot of hits!)

Discuss why you think these celebrity cults exist. Why would some people refuse to believe that their favorite star had actually died, despite proof surrounding the death? Perhaps someone in your group may want to play the devil's advocate and argue for reasons why one of these individuals is still alive. Does this belief in a deceased celebrity's present life speak to our culture's understanding (or misunderstanding) of death and humanity? Why might it be easier to believe a "normal" person has died than it is to believe a successful, famous, or infamous person has died?

You may have heard the old hymn, "Immortal, Invisible, God Only Wise." (If you don't know it, use the Internet or a hymnal to review the lyrics.) This hymn helps us to understand essential truths about God. But if God is *immortal*, and Jesus is part of God, how could Jesus have died?

1 On a scale of 1 to 10, how difficult would you rate this tough question? Explain your answer.

2 Who would you prefer to ask you this question: a child, your Unitarian friend, or the kind but staunch atheist in your workplace? Why? How would you form your answer in each case?

ENGAGE

DEATH IS NOT THE END

As Packer observes, it's only been recently that some segments of humanity have started to view death as the end of the person.

Historically, cultures realized that there is more to being a person than simply flesh and blood physicality.

In **Philippians 1:20-26**, Paul emphasized that death is not the end of the human experience. Read this text together.

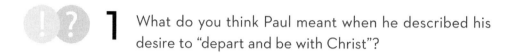

1   What do you think Paul meant when he described his desire to "depart and be with Christ"?

In his commentary on Philippians, Gordon Fee notes that "Paul understood death as a means into the Lord's immediate presence, which for him and countless thousands after him has been a comforting and encouraging prospect. Very likely he also expected such 'gain' to include consciousness, and for most believers, that too has been a matter of encouragement—although in this case such a conclusion goes beyond the certain evidence we possess from Paul himself."[1]

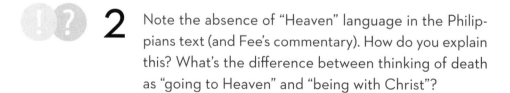

2   Note the absence of "Heaven" language in the Philippians text (and Fee's commentary). How do you explain this? What's the difference between thinking of death as "going to Heaven" and "being with Christ"?

In **1 Peter 3:18-22**, we learn something about what happened to Jesus while he was dead. Read this passage together. Historically, there has been a lot of speculation and debate surrounding this passage. "Did Jesus really go to Hell?" people have asked. But as Scot McKnight explains, the main emphasis in the text is that "Just as Jesus suffered as a righteous man and was vindicated, so too if the churches of Peter live righteously (as he has exhorted them to do), they will be vindicated and sit with Jesus in the presence of God."[2] For our purposes today—no matter how this text is interpreted—it definitively speaks to some existence of Christ after his death and before his resurrection.

DELVE DEEPER

If you'd like, explore these questions as a group or on your own:

One of the questions this study's discussion naturally leads to is: What does it mean to die?

How do you understand death? What cultural or emotional baggage does the word carry for you?

Read Romans 8:9-11 and 1 Corinthians 15:12-28. How does your view of death compare and contrast with what Paul said about death in these verses?

THE INCARNATION AND THE DEATH OF CHRIST

Packer uses the example of Shakespeare acting in his own plays as a metaphor for the incarnation. Read John's description of the incarnation in **John 1:1-18** together.

3 In your opinion, is the metaphor of a playwright acting in one of his or her own plays an appropriate way to explain the incarnation? Why or why not? Can you think of a better metaphor? Explain.

4 John 1 is one of the most literarily rich passages in the Bible—its poetry, imagery, rhythm, and word play are stunning. What examples of these do you see in this text? (Look for repetition, allusion to the Old Testament, comparison and contrast, simile and metaphor, lists, and cause and effect.)

5 Based only on this text, how can you describe the Word? What do you learn about it (him) from John 1? Explain.

In his article, Packer mentions some mysteries regarding the incarnation: "[H]ow, for instance, the sense of human and of divine identity meshed; how the Son controlled his divine powers so as not to overstep the limits of human finiteness; how entire dependence on his Father's leading for every word and deed made him the most unnerving initiative taker ever seen; and so on." Mysteries are part and parcel of Christianity; there are many mysteries surrounding major doctrinal issues of our faith, including the Trinity, creation, the virgin birth, and the new creation. It's important to remember that it's OK to not fully understand these truths.

6 What seems confusing or mysterious to you as you think about the incarnate Son dying on the cross? Be specific?

DELVE DEEPER

If you'd like, explore these questions as a group or on your own:

Hebrews 1:1-14 also alludes to the incarnation and addresses today's question. Read this passage, then consider the following questions: Using the literary analysis mentioned in the discussion of John 1 (see question 4), what sorts of word play do you see in this text? Why do you think Christ is compared to angels? What do you learn from this passage about Christ's divinity?

Colossians 1:15-20, an early Christian poem, touches on issues of the incarnation, the person of Christ, and the significance of his death. Read it along with Paul's additional remarks in **Colossians 1:15-23**.

7 How does Colossians 1:15-23 inform and enlighten your understanding of the incarnation and how it directly affects you?

CHRIST'S DEATH IS NOT THE END OF THE STORY

Some congregations have historically recited the following text together in their services: "Christ has died. Christ is risen. Christ will come again." These three sentences go together; we do not state one without the other and, similarly, we cannot adequately discuss the death of Christ (or even the question, "Did God die?") without understanding that Christ defeated death by rising from the dead.

8 Share examples of instances you've heard of or observed in our culture in which Christ's death is mentioned without discussion of his resurrection. (Consider movies, music, poems, books, plays, TV shows, and conversations with others.) Do you think this is ever OK? Why or why not?

Packer discusses how Christ's resurrection is the work of all three persons of the Trinity; Scripture points to this truth in **John 10:17, 18; Acts 13:30**; and **1 Peter 3:18**. Read these passages.

 9 In your opinion, does discussion of the Trinity's role in the resurrection simplify or complicate this mystery? Why?

Though Jesus' resurrection doesn't directly answer the difficult question we're examining in this study, it does provide very significant answers to other fundamental questions in our lives.

 10 What difference does Jesus' resurrection make in your everyday life? Be specific.

RESPOND

"God is dead." It's likely German philosopher Friedrich Nietzsche's most famous quote. Look more closely at what Nietzsche said:

> God is dead. God remains dead. And we have killed him. How shall we comfort ourselves, the murderers of all murderers? What was holiest and mightiest of all that the world has yet owned has bled to death under our knives: who will wipe this blood off us? What water is there for us to clean ourselves? What festivals of atonement, what sacred games shall we have to invent? Is not the greatness of this deed too great for us? Must we ourselves not become gods simply to appear worthy of it?[3]

Nietzsche did not write this to literally mean that a deity (God) had been alive and now was dead; rather, his point was that the traditional *idea* of "God" was dying in his time and culture. Nevertheless, Nietzsche's statement is quite provocative.

Within the context of your discussion today, how would you respond to Nietzsche's quote? How do you respond to current prevailing beliefs that Jesus died but did not rise from the dead?

REACT

During this study, how have you been personally impacted by your focus on Jesus' death and resurrection? Use the space below to reflect on how your exploration of the incarnation and Jesus' sacrifice has personally challenged you.

FOR FURTHER STUDY
BOOKS
- *Incarnation* by Alister McGrath (Fortress Press)
- *Incarnation and Resurrection* by Paul D. Molnar (Eerdmans)
- *Jesus and the Victory of God* by N. T. Wright (Augsburg Fortress)
- *The Kingdom and the Power: The Theology of Jürgen Moltmann* by Geiko Müller-Fahrenholz (Fortress Press)
- *The Resurrection of the Son of God* by N. T. Wright (Augsburg Fortress)
- *Scandalous: The Cross and the Resurrection of Jesus* by D. A. Carson (Crossway Books)

ONLINE ARTICLES
- "A New Way to be Human" by Kevin J. Corcoran, from *Books & Culture* (www.booksandculture.com/articles/2006/novdec/16.33.html)
- "A Resurrection That Matters" by J. R. Daniel Kirk, from *Christianity Today* (www.christianitytoday.com/ct/2010/april/10.37.html)

SONGS AND POEMS
- *Accompanied by Angels: Poems of the Incarnation* by Luci Shaw (Eerdmans)
- "And Can It Be That I Should Gain?" by Charles Wesley
- "Immortal, Invisible" by Walter Chalmers Smith

Wrap up the group time by reading together the following prayer (written by Thomas Cranmer in the sixteenth century):

Almighty God, which through your only begotten son Jesus Christ has overcome death, and opened unto us the gate of everlasting life; we humbly ask you, that, as by your special grace, preventing us, you put in our minds good desires, so by your continual help we may bring the same to good effect; through Jesus Christ our Lord who lives and reigns with you, one God, world without end, for ever and ever. Amen.[4]

STRETCH

Set aside time on your own soon after your small group meeting for worship and theological contemplation through historical church music.

Reading and singing Christian hymns has been one of the ways Christians throughout history have traditionally learned church doctrine and theology. There are many powerful hymns about the death and resurrection of Christ.

Take five to fifteen minutes each day this week to work on learning a hymn about the resurrection. Use an old hymnal or visit www .cyberhymnal.org to find the texts (and melodies) of one or more of the following hymns:

- "Christ the Lord Is Risen Today" by Charles Wesley
- "The Friend of Sinners Dies" by Isaac Watts
- "Our Lord Is Risen from the Dead" by Charles Wesley

As you read the hymn texts (and perhaps learn to sing them), prayerfully consider the following questions:

- What should my response be to the death of Christ?
- What should my response be to Christ's resurrection?
- How much of my own Christian life is centered around the resurrection of Christ? If necessary, what might I do to change this?

Study written by Joy-Elizabeth Lawrence. Joy-Elizabeth is a writer, actor, and staff member of Calvin College. In her graduate work, her studies focused on the theology of the body and the resurrection.

4

WHY WON'T GOD HEAL ME?
{ SUFFERING AND THE GIFTS OF GOD }

PREPARE

Before you meet with your small group, read this good question.
Then read the response article written by Nancy Ortberg.

GQ 4 Why has God answered others' prayers for healing, but not mine?

This is a complicated and tender question. Right now I'm praying for a close family friend who was diagnosed with terminal cancer five years ago. Two years later, he was "healed" (if you talked to his Christian friends), or in an "unexpected remission" (if you talked to his doctors). Today his cancer has returned and is unrelenting. He probably has two months to live. His Christian friends are confused, and his physicians are recommending hospice care.

Based on our own experience, there's so much we don't know about healing and prayer. Here's what we do know based on Scripture.

We're instructed to pray, but healing isn't guaranteed. James 5:14, 15 tells us to respond in prayer when someone is sick; "the prayer offered in faith will make the sick person well." But we also know from Scripture this isn't a guarantee.

In 2 Samuel 12, it says King David fasted and prayed for seven days for God to spare his dying child. In verse 22, David said, "Who knows? The LORD may be gracious to me and let the child live." When that wasn't the case, David got up and worshipped God anyway.

Healing miracles are relatively rare. *In the Bible, healing miracles seem like they occur on every page. But when you consider the Bible covers more than two thousand years of history, that's a relatively small amount of people who experienced direct physical healing. During his three and a half years of ministry, Jesus healed perhaps hundreds of deaf, blind, lame, and leprous people, but there were many more he didn't heal.*

> During his three and a half years of ministry, Jesus healed perhaps hundreds of deaf, blind, lame, and leprous people, but there were many more he didn't heal.

Also, biblical miracles tended to occur in clusters—during the Exodus from Egypt, in the times of the prophets, during Jesus' ministry, and with the start of the church. Author Brian Jones writes that we sometimes have a "distorted impression. God didn't deliver miracles every day like the morning newspaper. Most followers of God went their whole lives without witnessing a supernatural intervention on the part of heaven."

Healing miracles happen for reasons we don't always understand. *Jesus healed the paralytic on the mat when he saw the faith of the man's friends; he healed the Roman centurion's daughter based on that man's statements about Jesus (Matthew 8, 9). On the other hand, he healed the crippled woman on the Sabbath without her ever asking for help (Luke 13).*

Comparing answers to prayer—or a seeming lack of them—is unwise. *In John 21, the apostle Peter and Jesus are taking a post-resurrection walk on the beach. At one point in the conversation, Jesus tells Peter*

> Why one person is healed or spared suffering and another isn't, is often not ours to know.

about the kind of death Peter will experience, and it's not good news. Peter immediately turns behind him to look at the apostle John and says to Jesus, "What about him?" Jesus' reply is rather terse: "If I want him to remain alive until I return, what is that to you? You must follow me." Why one person is healed or spared suffering and another isn't, is often not ours to know.

My sixty-two year-old father was diagnosed with terminal cancer when my children were four, two, and newborn. After eighteen months of fervent prayers to God for my dad's healing, I stood at his bedside, stroked his head, whispered into his ear, and watched him leave this world.

Lazarus was healed. He was even raised from the dead. But then, ten or twenty years later, he died again.

In this fallen, broken world, death is inevitable. In the meantime, we pray. We pray and plead, and with open and upturned hands, we join with David in saying, "Who knows?"

Nancy Ortberg is a church leadership consultant and popular speaker. Formerly a teaching pastor at Willow Creek Community Church in Illinois, she now lives in California with her husband, John. "Playing Favorites" was originally published in the November/December 2005 issue of Today's Christian Woman *(Christianity Today International).*

LAUNCH

OPTIONAL EXERCISE

Your group may want to begin your meeting with this activity. You'll need **two dice, a CD or MP3 player**, and **six wrapped gift packages labeled with the numerals 1 through 6**; three of the gifts should contain a small prize (such as candy or some other treat the members of your group would find appealing); the other three should be empty.

Sit in a circle and assign one person the job of playing and randomly stopping the music. Everyone should pass the gifts around the circle until the music stops. When it does, one player should roll the dice (one die at a time).

The number on the first die that is rolled indicates which gift is in play. (For example, if a three is rolled on the first die, the person holding gift number 3 should get ready to do something.)

The number rolled on the second die indicates what should be done with the gift that is in play. Use the table of directions provided on the next page as your guide (or you can alter the directions as desired to suit your group). Once a gift has been opened, it is out of play. The game continues until all the gifts have been opened.

When the game is finished, talk about how it felt to "win" the gifts. Did you feel you deserved it? Did you feel excited? guilty? sorry for those who didn't win? How did it feel to *not* win a gift? Did you feel jealous? competitive? unlucky? Why?

If you were in charge of the rules of the game, what would you change? Why?

If you roll a . . .	then you should . . .
1	Do nothing at all. Resume play and keep passing gifts.
2	Pass the gift to the person on your **left** and let him or her roll the second die again.
3	Pass the gift to the person on your **right** and let him or her roll the second die again.
4	Pass the gift to the person on your **left**. He or she gets to open the gift and keep whatever is inside.
5	Pass the gift to the person on your **right**. He or she gets to open the gift and keep whatever is inside.
6	Open the gift and keep whatever is inside!

Sometimes praying for a miracle seems a bit like playing a game of luck. God's answers to our urgent concerns can feel as random as a roll of the dice. Sometimes we don't seem to hear from him at all, other times we seem to get a good word . . . only to have our hopes dashed, and other times we receive that precious gift from God we were hoping for. Both today and in biblical accounts, God seems to miraculously heal some and not others, without a consistent rhyme or reason.

 1 Have you ever prayed for miraculous healing for yourself or a loved one? If so, what happened? How did God's answer, whether positive or negative, affect your faith?

2 Do you believe God still does miracles today? Explain your perspective.

ENGAGE

HEALING ISN'T GUARANTEED

God is almighty. He is sovereign. He is omnipotent, omnipresent, and omniscient. God certainly doesn't need our advice or our assistance. He is so far beyond us that we're simply left in awe of him.

Job was a righteous man who endured terrible suffering; he lost his wealth and possessions, his health, and his family. Silently skim through **Job 38-41**. This passage is God's response to Job after Job has questioned God about his suffering.

 1 What do you think God's main point was in his words to Job? Try to sum up God's monologue to Job in one sentence, then discuss what this passage reveals about the character of God. (Keep in mind that you are looking at just one aspect of God; he has many other characteristics that are not revealed in this chapter.)

The Almighty God doesn't need us, but for some reason he invites us to participate with him in his activity here on earth. Scripture is very clear, in both the Old and New Testaments, that God wants us to pray—to call out to him for help and healing for ourselves and others. Read **James 5:13-16** together.

2 We are told to pray for each other and to expect a response from God. Why do you think God, who knows everything we need even before we ask, would tell us to pray for healing?

God wants us to pray, but it's equally clear that we are to surrender to his good and perfect will. He is faithful and will keep his promises, but we don't get to determine his answer to our prayers. Read Romans 12:1, 2.

DELVE DEEPER

If you'd like, explore this question as a group or on your own:

Scripture is full of promises about God answering our prayers. Read Matthew 7:7, 8 and Luke 11:5-13, and also review James 5:13-16.

How do we reconcile these passages with the fact that sometimes when we pray earnestly for healing, full of faith that God will answer, nothing seems to happen?

3 What is a living sacrifice? What does surrendering ourselves to God in this way have to do with prayer?

4 We're to pray according to God's will; and this passage tells us we can test and approve what God's will is by not conforming to the pattern of this world. What are some specific things we can do to be transformed by the renewing of our minds?

HEALING MIRACLES ARE RELATIVELY RARE

Miracles are not commonplace—not today and not in Bible times. In her article, Nancy Ortberg asserts that "Jesus healed perhaps hundreds of deaf, blind, lame, and leprous people, but there were many more he didn't heal."

5 As far as we know, Jesus performed miracles during just three years of his life. Imagine if he had devoted his entire life to healing people of their ailments! Sounds good . . . so why do you think healing people was *not* Jesus' top priority?

Not only did Jesus *not* spend his entire life on earth healing people, but he also sometimes passed by those who needed healing. For example, he once went by a pool where many disabled people would lie in hopes of being healed by miraculous powers. When Jesus was there, he did not stretch out his arm and declare all those people to be healed in one mighty stroke; he spoke to just one man. As far as we know, that man was the only person he healed that day. Read **John 5:1-9**.

6 Before healing him, Jesus asked the man if he wanted to be well. Why do you think Jesus asked such an obvious question?

7 Use your imagination to step into this story. What would it have been like to have been one of the other people waiting by the pool for healing and to see Jesus heal someone else? What thoughts or feelings do you think you would have experienced?

HEALING MIRACLES HAPPEN FOR REASONS WE DON'T ALWAYS UNDERSTAND

Ortberg describes various scenarios of healing—sometimes people are healed based on their faith, and other times they don't even ask for help. We all probably know of modern-day examples of good people dying and evil people prospering. God's healing doesn't seem to follow any pattern and, from our perspective, it can often seem unfair.

Read **Matthew 20:1-16** together.

DELVE DEEPER

If you'd like, explore these questions as a group or on your own:

Hebrews 12:7-11 makes it clear that sometimes we face hardships for our own good. Suffering, then, is not always evil; there may be times when God allows us to suffer rather than miraculously heal us because that suffering is an avenue of spiritual growth.

What's the difference between discipline and punishment? What are some specific ways to respond to hardships so that we might grow in righteousness?

8 One of the essential characteristics of God is that he is just; why then do you think Jesus told this story to illustrate how God is not concerned with being "fair" when it comes to our salvation?

Roger Hahn, in *Matthew: A Commentary for Bible Students*, explains why the landowner in the parable above, who represents God, is *not* being unfair. "The point is not injustice to the person who worked all day but the goodness the landowner wanted to extend to the worker hired last. . . . Jesus' parable speaks specifically of the generosity of God's grace. . . . No one deserves the benefits of the Kingdom. Some have worked longer and harder than others, but the reward of the messianic banquet is offered to all without regard to the work they have done."[1]

9 Take a moment to reflect on whether *anyone* deserves miraculous healing. Scripture makes it clear that we all deserve death (Romans 3:23). Why then does God heal anyone at all? What does this teach us about the character of God?

Ortberg ends her article with these poignant words: "In this fallen, broken world, death is inevitable. In the meantime, we pray. We pray and plead, and with open and upturned hands, we join with David in saying, 'Who knows?'"

10 Since we can't possibly know how God will answer our pleading, why is it comforting to bring our needs before the Lord? What does the process of prayer do for us? What does it do for God?

RESPOND

It can be hurtful and insensitive (as well as theologically dangerous) to offer pat answers or Christian clichés to a hurting person who's wondering why God allows him or her to continue to suffer. What meaningful responses *can* we provide to suffering loved ones? What types of "answers" should we avoid? Discuss this together.

REACT

Take a moment to write your response to these questions in the space below: How should we pray when we are in need of a miracle? Where's the line between making demands of God to fit our will and believing firmly in his power while reminding him of his promises?

Sit together for a time of silent group-prayer. Quietly ask God to help you each receive his grace, no questions asked. Pray that the Holy Spirit will help you to accept his will. Then together pray aloud Jesus' words from the Garden of Gethsemane (Luke 22:42): "Not my will, but yours be done." Amen.

FOR FURTHER STUDY
BOOKS

- *Are Miraculous Gifts for Today?* by Wayne Grudem and Stanley Gundry, eds. (Zondervan)
- *The God of Miracles* by C. John Collins (Crossway Books)
- *God Still Heals* by James L. Garlow (Wesleyan Publishing House)
- *If God is Good* by Randy Alcorn (Multnomah)
- *Holding on to Hope* by Nancy Guthrie (Tyndale)
- *Miracles* by C. S. Lewis (HarperOne)
- *Miracles Do Happen* by Briege McKenna (Charis Books)
- *A Place of Healing* by Joni Eareckson Tada (Cook)
- *Why Me?—Straight Talk About Suffering* by Lawrence W. Wilson (Beacon Hill Press)

ONLINE RESOURCES

- "Do Miracles Happen Today?" video by John Piper (www.youtube.com/watch?v=Bgs38_x1XJg)
- "Do Miracles of Healing Happen Today?" from John Mark Ministries (jmm.aaa.net.au/articles/9432.htm)
- "Do Miracles Still Happen Today?" from Faith Talk Ministries (www.faithtalkministries.com/apps/articles/default.asp?articleid=52846&columnid=4824)
- "The End of Suffering" by Scott Cairns, from ChristianityToday.com (www.christianitytoday.com/ct/2010/february/25.62.html)

STRETCH

Set aside time on your own soon after your small group meeting for Bible research.

A word study is an excellent way to get the big picture of a certain topic in Scripture; use this method to engage the subject of miraculous healing in greater depth.

1. Get a notepad, a pen or pencil, and a concordance of your choice. You can use the concordance found at the back of a study Bible, a more extensive concordance, or an online concordance (such as using the search function at www.BibleGateway.com).
2. Write this word at the top of the page: *Heal.*
3. List all the passages you find with the word *heal* and its variants (*healed, healing,* and so on).
4. Thoughtfully and prayerfully, read the passages you've listed (including their surrounding context).
5. Optional: Use additional Bible study tools to look up the word in Greek and Hebrew and to examine a Bible dictionary entry for the word.

6. Write a brief paragraph summing up what you've learned about the word, and more importantly, about God and your relationship with him.

If you'd like, invest additional time in this exercise, perhaps continuing your word study over the course of several weeks.

Study written by Heather Gemmen Wilson. Heather is a best-selling author and award-winning international speaker (www.heathergemmen.com). She is married to a pastor, and together they have six children.

DOES DIVISION DISCREDIT THE CHURCH?

{ LIVING IN THE UNITY CHRIST PRAYED FOR }

Before you meet with your small group, read this good question. Then read the response article written by Bruce Shelley.

GQ 5 Why do we have denominations when Jesus prayed for the unity of believers? **Don't our divisions discredit the church?**

Many people see the existence of denominations as a blot against the church's witness to unity. So they are surprised to learn that denominations were created with quite the opposite intent—to make unity in the church possible. To understand this counterintuitive historical reality, one has to look back 400 years to the century following the Protestant Reformation.

The Reformers had glimpsed a coming day by insisting that the true church could never be identified exclusively with a particular institution (contra Constantine in the fourth century). Still, the Reformers failed to follow this lead; like the Catholics, the Protestants continued to believe that Christian truth held societies together and that only one side in a religious conflict could have the truth. Nonconformity could *not be tolerated, and the truth was worth fighting for. And fight they did.*

It was not until sheer exhaustion—not victory for any party—brought an end to the religiously motivated Thirty Years War (with the signing of the Peace of Westphalia in 1648) that something of a truce over territorial religion began to take shape. This truce allowed Calvinism to join Lutheranism and Catholicism as a recognized expression of the Christian faith. But this new "peace" retained the territorial concept—those who weren't Calvinist, Lutheran, or Catholic, such as the nonterritorial Anabaptists, or who lived in the wrong territory, continued to be persecuted.

At about the same time in England, the first clear philosophy of denominations was being articulated by the Independents (Congregationalists), who represented the minority voice at the Westminster Assembly (1642-49). In contrast to the majority who held to Presbyterian principles and expressed these convictions in the Westminster Confession of Faith, the Independents followed congregational principles. Keenly aware of the dangers of "dividing the godly Protestant party," these "Dissenting Brethren of Westminster" looked for some way to express Christian unity even in disagreement.

The result was a denominational theory of the church that was based on the following principles: First, considering the human inability always to see the truth clearly, differences of opinion about the outward form of the church are inevitable. Second, even though these differences do not involve fundamentals of the faith, they are not matters of indifference. Third, since no church has a final and full grasp of divine truth, the true church of Christ can never be fully represented by any single ecclesiastical structure. Finally, the mere fact of separation does not of itself constitute schism. It is possible to be divided at many points and still be united in Christ.

Though drafted in old England, these principles found their fullest expression in New England. To be profitable, the American colonies needed people to settle the land, and the promise of religious toleration provided a powerful incentive. Also, many of those who came from Europe brought with them the lesson of the Thirty Years War—that the price of enforced religious conformity was too high.

Inevitably, immigration patterns and the lack of a state religion led to the flowering of a multiplicity of religious groups—traditional and novel—living side by side in the New World. In such a setting, the denominational theory seemed a plan from heaven. "Denominationalism" came to be set against "sectarianism," which denoted groups claiming the authority of Christ and truth for themselves alone and believing that they alone constituted the true body of Christ. Against this exclusive connotation, denomination became an inclusive term, implying that any Christian group "denominated" by a particular name was but one member of a larger group—the church.

> It is possible to be divided at many points and still be united in Christ.

As we know, the denominational concept prevailed—not because it was considered ideal, but because it was better than any alternative the preceding years and centuries had offered.

At a personal level, many of us have at times experienced denominations as sources of conflict, not unity, proving that no organizational solution can of itself fulfill the oneness for which Jesus prayed. Organized unity is only possible if there is an experienced unity, a oneness of spirit or attitude. The apostle Paul once said of those who differed with him, "Christ is preached and in this I rejoice." Apparently it is possible to find our unity in Christ and the gospel even as we agree to disagree over some finer points of doctrine and traditional practices.

Bruce Shelley was a church history professor at Denver Seminary and the author of over thirty books. "Denominations: Divided We Stand" was first published in the September 1998 issue of Christianity Today.

LAUNCH

OPTIONAL EXERCISE

Your group may want to begin your meeting with this activity. You'll need **paper** and **pens** or **pencils**.

It's time to let your spiritual gift of comedy out of the box! Divide your small group into two . . . now start a couple of new church denominations. Just kidding! But seriously folks, give each of the two groups the task of completing this classic comedy line: How many _____ does it take to change a light bulb?

But instead of "blondes" or "Chicago Bears fans" in the blank, insert various denominations or church movements, like evangelicals, charismatics, Baptists, Presbyterians, emerging church followers, and so on.

Keep things lighthearted, fun, and definitely not mean-spirited. And laugh at yourselves—be sure to include your own denomination, church, or small group in your comedic efforts!

Together in your smaller team, try to come up with about five light-bulb changing jokes. After five minutes, gather back together and take turns sharing your comedy stylings with the full group. (Pity laughter is welcome!)

Next, discuss with your group members why you laughed or winced when you created and listened to the denominational jokes.

Take just two minutes to brain-storm as a group, listing by name all the Christian churches you can think of in your town or community. How high is the number?

It's tough enough for a Christian to move into a new community and try to find a church, but just imagine what this denominational smorgas-bord looks like to an unbelieving or not-sure-yet world.

DELVE DEEPER

If you'd like, explore these questions as a group or on your own:

Disunity can hurt the church's witness; conversely, unity among believers can profoundly demonstrate the gospel message. Read about the experience of the newborn church in Acts 2:42-47.

How have you seen church unity draw people to the gospel? What role has a healthy, vibrant, and unified Christian community played in your own faith commitment or spiritual growth?

1 How do you think non-Christians in your community view this diversity of churches and denominations? (If you've had conversations with non-Christian friends about this, share their observations.)

2 Imagine interviewing members of different churches in your community. Why would they say they went to their particular church rather than to your church?

ENGAGE

DIVISION CAN HURT THE CHURCH'S WITNESS

On the night of the Last Supper, before Jesus was arrested, he taught his disciples about servanthood, suffering, and the Holy Spirit. Then Jesus prayed for his disciples and for the future church. Read his prayer in **John 17:20-26.**

1 If Christian love and unity proclaims the gospel (17:23), then what message does division or disunity send to the world? Share examples of disunity you've observed that you think discredit the church or mar the gospel message.

"Many people see the existence of denominations as a blot against the church's witness to unity," Bruce Shelley observed in his article. Consider this reflection on denominations from pastor and author Frederick Buechner: "The question is not, Are you a Baptist? But, What kind of Baptist? It is not, Are you a member of the Presbyterian church? But Which Presbyterian church? A town with a population of less than five hundred may have churches of three or four denominations. . . . All the duplication of effort and waste of human resources. All the confusion about what The Church is, both within the ranks and without. All the counterproductive competition . . . you don't know whether to burst into laughter or into tears."[1]

This is not just a new phenomenon; denominations have been around for hundreds of years and division has been part of the church since its inception.

Read Paul's response to division among the Christians in Corinth in **1 Corinthians 1:10-18**.

2 What comparisons to the modern-day church does this passage bring to mind for you?

3 How would you summarize Paul's appeal to the church in your own words? What's the basis for this appeal?

UNITY IN CHRIST CAN BRIDGE DIVISION

We are right to be concerned about the damage denominational lines can have on our witness to the world, but what's perhaps even worse is when particular church groups claim to have the monopoly on the truth and view themselves as the one and only "true" body of Christ. In contrast to this type of sectarianism, Shelley explained that, from a church history perspective, denominations were intended to "make unity in the church possible." He went on

DELVE DEEPER

If you'd like, explore these questions as a group or on your own:

Questions of Christian practice and theological nuance were not the only issues that divided early Christians; personal conflicts arose and believers struggled to get along. Despite Paul and Barnabas's gallant fight for Christian unity based on the gospel of grace, a serious conflict arose between the two of them. Read what happened in Acts 15:36-41.

Ironically, the division between Paul and Barnabas led to a doubling of missionary efforts as they both went out (with new companions) to share the good news. How can God use division for good? Consider examples from your own life, community, or church history.

Paul wrote his first letter to the Corinthians some time after this falling out with his ministry partner Barnabas. How does your knowledge of his conflict with Barnabas affect your understanding of Paul's teachings about unity in Christ in 1 Corinthians 1:10? Explain.

to explain that "*denomination* [was meant to be] an inclusive term, implying that any Christian group 'denominated' by a particular name was but one member of a larger group—the church." This ability to find unity in Christ, despite our differences, can be a powerful testimony to the world.

The early church experienced significant division over key issues of Christian practice, yet they were able to cultivate harmony at the Council at Jerusalem without compromising on the truth. The church in Antioch had run up against teachers who were adding to the gospel of grace. "Unless you are circumcised, . . . you cannot be saved," they preached (Acts 15:1), adding requirements from the law of Moses to the gospel of Jesus.

Tensions arose as Gentiles professed faith in Christ and entered a community made up of Jewish followers of Jesus whose entire lives had been enveloped in the Law. Would the new Gentile believers need to in essence become Jewish to be Christian?

The potential for conflict was high as Paul and Barnabas went to Jerusalem to address this issue before the apostles and elders. Read **Acts 15:1-31**.

4 What lessons for the church today are there in the Jerusalem Council's resolution process?

5 What does this passage tell you about the value we should place on unity? on truth? Explain.

Though the Council at Jerusalem found a solution, church history (and likely our own personal experience) demonstrates that there are also times when the deeply held personal or theological convictions of earnest, Christ-focused people simply differ too significantly for them to find agreement.

6 How are we to respond when our efforts toward unity are in tension with our personal or theological convictions? Are there times when these two priorities are incompatible—when one must be abandoned in order to achieve the other? Explain.

7 When does division mean disunity? When might it actually allow for unity?

CHRISTIAN UNITY REQUIRES OUR EFFORT AND HUMILITY

Churches can be difficult, painful communities. We've all experienced this in some way: controlling leaders, wounded people who hurt others, miscommunication, differing visions for ministry, awkward social interactions—the list goes on and on and on. But these messy and often dysfunctional communities can also be sources of real joy and help.

Shelley's words remind us that "Organized unity is only possible if there is an experienced unity, a oneness of spirit or attitude." This is true not just about local church families, but about the broader body of Christ; it takes intentional effort to cultivate a spirit of unity in our mind-set about other denominations. Shelley asserted that "it is possible to find our unity in Christ and the gospel even as we agree to disagree over some finer points of doctrine and traditional practices."

8 Tell about a time you experienced unity, despite differences, with someone who was part of a different denomination or church movement. How was that unity possible?

Read how Paul and James describe unity—and how it is achieved—in **Romans 14:13, 19; 15:1, 2; Ephesians 4:2-6,** and **James 3:13–4:12.**

9 Paul urges us to "make every effort" toward unity (Romans 14:19, Ephesians 4:3). What types of efforts are outlined in the above passages? What other actions, attitudes, or choices are necessary to work toward unity with other Christians?

10 What, for you, is the most challenging part of working toward unity with other Christians? Why?

RESPOND

In light of all you've talked about, how would you answer a friend who says, "You Christians can't even get along with each other. How can I believe in Jesus' message if you all seem to disagree about it?" What truths, ideas, or examples would you share with your friend?

REACT

How do you feel God wants you to grow or change in regard to unity within the church? What is one step you will take to respond to God's Word in this area? Write your thoughts below.

Close your time together by re-reading John 17:20, 21 in an attitude of prayer. As you do, keep in mind that Jesus prayed these words for his future church—and that includes you. Use Jesus' prayer as a launching point for your own time of group prayer, asking God to help you seek a greater Christian unity that results in a powerful witness to the world.

STRETCH

Set aside time on your own soon after your small group meeting for a time of personal prayer.

Author and philosopher Francis Schaeffer once wrote that, when it comes to preaching the message of Christ, "We must not forget the final apologetic. The world has a right to look upon us as we, as true Christians, come to practical differences and it should be able to observe that we do love each other. Our love must have a form that the world may observe; it must be seeable."[2]

How are you doing in this area? How do you relate to Christians with whom you've got "practical differences"?

Identify a specific Christian you know (from your church, community, or family) with whom you have a hard time getting along. Write that person's name on a scrap of paper.

Next identify a church in your community that's not like yours—a denomination or group with whom you have significant differences about worship style, Christian practice, or (nonessential) theological beliefs and biblical interpretations. Add the church's name to the piece of paper.

Now spend time praying for that person and that church. Don't pray a cursory, short prayer; devote at least ten minutes to focused, earnest intercession. Pray for their spiritual growth and well-being; ask God to work powerfully through them to share the gospel with a lost world. Honestly acknowledge your differences with them and invite God to convict you of sin in your attitude or behavior toward them. Ask God to help you find unity with them; rely on his power to help you live out a love for them that is "seeable."

FOR FURTHER STUDY
BOOKS

- *Community and Growth* by Jean Vanier (Paulist)
- *A History of the Christian Church* by Williston Walker, et al. (Scribner)
- *Life Together* by Dietrich Bonhoeffer (HarperOne)
- *The Mark of the Christian* by Francis A. Schaeffer (InterVarsity Press)
- *The Mosaic of Christian Belief* by Roger E. Olson (InterVarsity Academic)
- "The Purity & Unity of the Church" in *Systematic Theology* by Wayne Grudem (Zondervan)
- *Turning Points* by Mark A. Noll (Baker Academic)

ONLINE ARTICLES

- "Christian Unity & the Cross," sermon by John Piper (www.desiringgod.org/resource-library/sermons/christian-unity-and-the-cross)
- "A Common Bond" by Rick Atchley and Bob Russell, from *The Lookout* (www.lookoutmag.com/articles/articledisplay.asp?id=161)
- "Why Should I Care About Unity?" by Paul Thigpen, from *Discipleship Journal* (www.navpress.com/magazines/archives/article.aspx?id=11730)

Study written by Kyle White. Kyle White is the founding director of Neighbors' House, an outreach to at-risk students in DeKalb County, Illinois. He is a freelance writer, frequent contributor to Christian BibleStudies.com, and the author of *Wisconsin River of Grace*.

6

WHAT SCRIPTURES STILL APPLY TODAY?

{ DISCOVERING HOW SCRIPTURE SPOKE IN THE PAST IS CRITICAL TO HEARING IT NOW }

PREPARE

Before you meet with your small group, read this good question. Then read the response article written by Craig S. Keener. (If you're able, also read **1 Corinthians 8–10** before your small group meeting.)

GQ 6 Most evangelicals don't ask women to wear a head covering when praying or expect slaves to obey masters—because "that was just their culture." Yet many do forbid women to preach—because "this is a spiritual principle not bound by culture." **How do I determine which biblical directives are culture-bound and which are not?**

Everyone would agree that Paul's request for Timothy to pick up his cloak in Troas was a one-time request not addressed to all Christians always and everywhere.

We also agree that biblical guidance to slaves addressed a specific cultural context and does not require us to reinstitute the practice so we can obey it. But we still disagree over women's ordination and even the head covering. Why? Because distinguishing transcultural principles from the cul-

tural setting in which the Bible communicates them is sometimes difficult.

Some students I taught in Nigeria affirmed the practice of the women's head covering as described in 1 Corinthians 11. "The Bible commands it," they noted. But when I asked why none of them had greeted me with a holy kiss that day, they laughed. The temptation is to appeal to "common sense" as to what is time-bound and what is not. But our "common sense" often proves time-bound as well. In a sense, everything in the Bible has a cultural setting; yet everything in the Bible also remains God's Word. God inspired the biblical writers to address the issues of their day, and we will hear God's message when we properly apply their message to analogous situations today. This requires several steps. I will apply them here to the question of the head covering.

First, we need to understand what issues the biblical writers were addressing. The text itself helps us reconstruct some of these issues, but we can fill in many other gaps by learning what cultural matters the first readers took for granted (and therefore did not need to hear explained). Various tools, such as the International Standard Bible Encyclopedia or the IVP Bible Background Commentaries, can help in reconstructing these backgrounds. We have learned that people covered their heads for various reasons, but women in the Eastern Mediterranean especially covered their hair when they got married. Because many people considered hair the chief element of female beauty, they believed that only a husband should view his wife's hair. Many thus associated uncovered hair with seduction. More wealthy women, however, paid a lot for their stylish hair fashions and often left their hair uncovered, possibly exacerbating tension between wealthier and poorer women.

Second, we need to examine how the biblical writer deals with the contemporary issue he addresses. Granted that the author addresses a specific issue of his day, what transcultural principles guide his argument? Paul certainly would oppose behavior that could appear seductive; he also warns against bringing dishonor on one's family. Paul also opposed ostentation and class division in the church.

The third (and most difficult) step is determining which situations today are truly analogous to the biblical situations. For example, could the principles Paul uses to support head coverings in Corinth ever require some women not to wear head coverings today? What if head coverings themselves become ostentatious objects of attention or attraction (like other adornments in 1 Timothy 2:9)? What if one lived in a culture where wearing such coverings proved more of a stumbling block than not wearing them? For example, in West Philadelphia, we usually associate such coverings with Islam.

Distinguishing transcultural principles from the cultural setting in which the Bible communicates them is sometimes difficult.

The difficulty in finding accurate analogies becomes greater as our cultures move further and further from the biblical cultures. Yet one can trace different cultures even in the Bible: an ideal ancient Israelite woman might sell clothing in the market (Proverbs 31); in the Greek culture of Ephesus, however, an ideal matron might provide a better witness at home (1 Timothy 5:14). Is it possible that on some issues more than one practice is acceptable, depending on the culture we are addressing?

Doubtless, interpreters and faith communities will differ on specific cases of what is analogous and what is not, but most will agree on the principles of interpretation outlined above. That we sometimes come to different conclusions using the same methods reinforces the need for charity on secondary issues and reliance on the Holy Spirit to guide us into all truth. But it also draws our attention to the central messages that always remain clear in Scripture, such as the saving message of the gospel and basic ethical issues. Much of Scripture simply contextualized these central points for their first readers' cultures, giving us examples for how we should contextualize the central biblical message for our cultures today.

Craig S. Keener is a Professor of New Testament at Palmer Theological Seminary and author of The IVP Bible Background Commentary: New Testament. *"Veils, Kisses, and Biblical Commands" was first published in the October 1998 issue of* Christianity Today.

LAUNCH

OPTIONAL EXERCISE

Your group may want to begin your meeting with this activity. Set out a **large bowl of French fries** and **six smaller bowls for condiments**. Fill some of the smaller bowls with dips that are familiar to North Americans, such as ketchup, chili, and a nacho cheese dip. Then fill the other bowls with dips that are more common for Europeans or Africans to eat with fries: mayonnaise, vinegar, and hot sauce.

Take time to all eat the fries and sample the various dips, keeping in mind that each dip represents cultural and regional tastes.

Talk together about which flavors you each enjoyed the most and enjoyed the least. As you compare your opinions, reflect together on how our tastes are formed by the families, places, and cultures that we come from. What are some examples of other foods that *you* enjoy that others from different families or cultures might find unappealing?

Though we rarely acknowledge it, we make a cross-cultural journey whenever we open our Bibles. It took more than a thousand years and dozens of writers to record the book that we now call the Bible. The works of these writers represent a variety of genres, including history, poetry, prophecy, letters, and apocalyptic literature. God spoke his Word to the original hearers of Scripture in forms and languages that applied to them. The timeless words of God we read today were originally given in specific times and to particular people.

This is good news for us. As Gordon Fee and Douglas Stuart write in *How to Read the Bible for All Its Worth*, "Precisely because God chose to speak in the context of real human history, we may take courage that these same words will speak again and again in our own 'real' history."[1]

1 Create a list of some passages where you've noticed the "real" history of the Bible affecting how we interpret Scripture. Use these questions: a) What are some images and events in the Bible that you have trouble making sense of because of the cultural disconnect between the ancient world and today? b) What are some passages in which important commandments and theological ideas are joined with culturally rooted applications?

So how can we hear God's Word for us today as we read scriptural passages that are rooted in another time and place? In this study, we'll use **1 Corinthians 8-10** as a case study for how to implement several key principles of biblical interpretation.

ENGAGE

UNDERSTANDING THE BIBLE REQUIRES CULTURAL AWARENESS

In 1 Corinthians 8, Paul addressed the habit that some Corinthian Christians had of eating meat that had been offered to idols. Very few Americans have ever been in an identical situation. But at the time Paul wrote—about two decades after Jesus ascended into Heaven—few Christians would have been in this situation either. In fact, in 1 Corinthians 8-10, Paul was doing something that Christians still do today. He was reading a cultural situation (eating idol meat) in light of the story of God's work in Jesus Christ (God calling a community of people away from idols to himself).

Read **1 Corinthians 10:14-22** and then consider how an awareness of both the broader message of Scripture on the topic and an understanding of the culture of the ancient world can open up to us God's message for the Corinthians then—and for us today.

1. How does God's Word address idols in the Old Testament? And how would we expect Paul, whose message is in agreement with the Old Testament, to respond to church members eating meat offered to idols? Brainstorm together and create a list of the various ways in which the Bible talks about idols. (Consider some texts that come to mind on your own, as well as several of these: Exodus 20:4-6; Exodus 32; 1 Samuel 15:22, 23; Psalm 31:6; Isaiah 44:9-20; Jeremiah 10:14-16; Acts 17:16-28; 1 Corinthians 10:1-7.)

2 What do you know about idols and idolatry in the first-century Greco-Roman world that might be relevant to understanding the cultural situation Paul is addressing in 1 Corinthians 10? List your thoughts. (These passages may give you additional insights: Acts 15:19-21; 17:16, 22, 23; 19:17-20, 23-41; 1 Corinthians 8:1-13.)

Many of the clues for how to understand the cultural situation in 1 Corinthians 10 are already in the Bible. If we're willing to consider the Old Testament's teachings on idolatry and combine them with the descriptions we're given of Greek cities and paganism in the New Testament, we will be well on our way toward Craig Keener's first suggestion: "We need to understand what issues the biblical writers were addressing."

DELVE DEEPER

If you'd like, explore this question as a group or on your own:

Sometimes, even after searching the Old Testament, New Testament, and history books, we might still end up scratching our heads. For example, read 1 Corinthians 11:4, 5 and then look at 1 Corinthians 14:33-35. In the first passage, Paul assumed that women play an active role in worship (praying and prophesying). This comes right after Paul commended them for maintaining the traditions he passed on to them (11:2). But just a few chapters later, Paul forbade women from speaking in church. *Huh?*

From your experience, what value can we draw from passages that continue to perplex us?

3 Create a summary statement as a group by completing this sentence: In light of the contexts of the Old Testament and the first-century Greco-Roman world, we would describe the problem with eating meat sacrificed to idols by saying that . . .

UNDERSTANDING BRINGS APPRECIATION

We can be thankful that Paul did not address the situation of certain Christians eating idol meat by simply saying, "Stop it." Instead, Scripture tells us not only what to do but also how to think about our actions.

4 Briefly look over the entire section in which Paul addressed idol meat and use the table below to list the various ways in which he helped his original audience think about their actions.

Read 1 Corinthians	Ask
8:4-13	What was Paul's main concern about idol meat in this section?
Notes:	
9	Paul gave many examples about how he had denied himself certain rights and privileges. How does this connect to his argument in chapter 8?
Notes:	

10:1-11	What was Paul's main point about idol meat in this section?
Notes:	
10:14-22	What was Paul's main point about idol meat in this section?
Notes:	

How would you sum up in your own words the main concerns raised by the Scriptures presented in the table?

When we encounter passages that are so bound to a particular time and place, we are tempted to go one of two extremes: First, we might say, "That was only applicable back then," and live as if those passages had no message for us today. Or, second, we might say, "We have to live out the exact instruction of that text," and then we end up trying to recreate the living conditions of the ancient world in the twenty-first century.

5 In your view, what would we miss if we ignored how 1 Corinthians 8–10 teaches us to think and act regarding meat sacrificed to idols?

6 On the other hand, what would we miss if we insisted on a very rigid interpretation of 1 Corinthians 8–10— one that limited what it had to teach us only to situations that included pagan temples and idol meat?

UNDERSTANDING BRINGS APPLICATION

Keener asserts that a faithful interpretation of God's Word for today will find modern situations in which the biblical principles still apply.

Many interpreters who read 1 Corinthians 8–10 say that at the very least Paul's instructions from that passage can guide our thoughts about Christian freedom. For instance, certain Christians drink alcohol, while other Christians are deeply troubled and even tempted to sin when they're in the presence of alcohol. Paul teaches us that bringing down a fellow Christian this way is the same as sinning against Christ (1 Corinthians 8:12)!

In their book, *Introduction to Biblical Interpretation*, William Klein, Craig Blomberg, and Robert Hubbard write about applying Scripture to life today in this way: "[F]aithful application of the Bible to new contexts requires that we become as earnest in our study of the contemporary world as we are of Scripture itself."[2]

> ### DELVE DEEPER
>
> If you'd like, explore these questions as a group or on your own:
>
> Turn to James 4:13-17. In this passage, James shed light on a cultural habit of his time (a popular saying), but he understood even a simple way of speaking as something that reflected a deeper problem in the human heart. Read the passage aloud.
>
> Brainstorm together: What are some cultural habits today (ways of speaking or assumptions about how to live) that reflect deeper truths about the spiritual values of our culture? What are some passages of Scripture that might address these cultural assumptions?

7 Look back at the principles that you have noted from reviewing 1 Corinthians 8–10 (question 4). What might be some situations in our contemporary world in which we could apply Paul's principles?

8 Make your application personal. Share about a time in your own life in which the message of this passage has applied to you, even if the particular situation (eating meat sacrificed to idols) did not.

9 In light of all you've read, what do we gain when we allow the Bible to speak through culture and put our effort into studying how it does this? Explain.

RESPOND

Imagine that a friend or colleague comes to you and says, "I'm confused. Most of the commands of Scripture come out of a Middle Eastern or Greek culture and they only really make sense in that kind of a context. Plus it's ancient! How can Christians in the twenty-first century claim that the Bible is a guide for their lives?" Discuss this question as a group and together come up with a thorough response.

REACT

Privately think about these questions: Are there passages in Scripture that you've struggled to find applicable to your life? What's one passage of Scripture that you'd like to explore in greater depth in order to find out how God's Word speaks through that passage? Write your thoughts here:

Divide up into groups of three or four. Share with the others in your new group what you would like prayer for, and in particular what passage or topic you would like to spend more time studying in order to better understand it. End your time by praying together in your groups of three and four.

STRETCH

Set aside time on your own soon after your small group meeting for a time of personal Bible study.

Block out an evening for personal study of a difficult Bible passage that you would like to understand better. Assemble some good resources for studying the Bible (for example, a few different English translations of your passage, one or two good commentaries, a concordance). You can find many of these online (for example, at www.Bible Gateway.com), at a local library, or you can borrow some books from your pastor or church library. Use these steps as a guide:

1. Begin by praying: Ask God to open your eyes to the message of Scripture. Confess your inadequacy to determine the meaning of the Bible on your own.
2. Read through your passage several times. Read the chapters before and after your passage, too. If the book that your passage is in is short, read the whole book of the Bible.
3. Underline important words and phrases.
4. Write down specific questions you have. (For example, "Why does the author use this particular word?" or "How does this connect to what comes before? How does it lead in to what follows?")
5. Try to answer those questions by looking to the surrounding context. If you need to look further, turn to your concordance.

FOR FURTHER STUDY
BOOKS
- *The Blue Parakeet: Rethinking How You Read the Bible* by Scot McKnight (Zondervan)
- *Eat This Book: A Conversation in the Art of Spiritual Reading* by Eugene Peterson (Eerdmans)
- *How to Read the Bible Book by Book* by Gordon Fee and Douglas Stuart (Zondervan)
- *How to Read the Bible for All Its Worth* by Gordon Fee and Douglas Stuart (Zondervan)
- *The IVP Bible Background Commentary: New Testament* by Craig Keener (InterVarsity)
- *The IVP Bible Background Commentary: Old Testament* by John Walton (InterVarsity)
- *The Zondervan Encyclopedia of the Bible* by Merrill Tenney and Moises Silva (Zondervan)

ONLINE ARTICLES
- "The Bible and Tomorrow's World" by N. T. Wright (www.ntwrightpage.com/)
- "The Habits of Highly Effective Bible Readers" from *Christian History & Biography* at ChristianityToday.com (www.christianity today.com/ch/2003/issue80/4.9.html)
- "The Heresy of Application," from *Leadership* journal at ChristianityToday.com (www.christianitytoday.com/le/1997/fall/7l4020.html)

Write down preliminary answers. This is where you should spend most of your time.

6. Now turn to your commentaries. What do those writers say? What new questions do they raise for you?

7. Answer this question if you can: What was the impact of this passage on its original audience?

8. Once you have an idea of what the text said in its original context and the logic behind that text, make the transition to your world. What would it look like to apply this text today in a way that is faithful to its original setting?

9. Write a short summary of what you learned during your study and what questions still remain.

End your time by praying and thanking God for the things he revealed to you—even if you still have questions when you're finished.

Study written by Christopher Blumhofer. His writings have appeared in *Leadership* journal, *Relevant*, and BuildingChurchLeaders.com.

• NOTES •

SESSION 1

1. Moby, *18* (Little Idiot Music/Warner-Tamerlane Publishing, 2002), liner notes essay.

2. Douglas Groothuis, *Truth Decay: Defending Christianity Against the Challenges of Postmodernism* (Downers Grove: InterVarsity Press, 2000), 27-28.

3. Huston Smith, *The World's Religions* (New York: HarperOne, 2009), 385-386.

4. G. K. Chesterton, *Orthodoxy* (San Francisco: Ignatius Press, 1995) 36-37.

5. Ibid., 39.

6. James W. Sire, *The Universe Next Door: A Basic Worldview Catalog*, Third Edition (Downers Grove: InterVarsity Press, 1997), 195.

7. Ibid, 193.

8. Anthony C. Thiselton, "Truth," in *The New International Dictionary of New Testament Theology*, ed. Colin Brown (Grand Rapids: Zondervan, 1975), 893.

9. Blaise Pascal, *Pensées*, trans. A. J. Krailsheimer, (New York: Penguin Books, 1966), 54.

SESSION 2

1. Alister E. McGrath, ed., *The Christian Theology Reader* (Oxford: Blackwell, 1995), 220.

2. Donald G. Bloesch, *Essentials of Evangelical Theology Volume 1: God, Authority, and Salvation* (Peabody: Prince Press, 1978), 26.

3. Jürgen Moltmann, *The Crucified God* (Minneapolis: Fortress Press, 1993), 205.

SESSION 3

1. Gordon Fee, *New International Commentary on the New Testament: Paul's Letter to the Philippians* (Grand Rapids: Eerdmans, 1995), 149.

2. Scot McKnight, *The NIV Application Commentary: 1 Peter,* (Grand Rapids: Zondervan, 1996), 215.

3. Friedrich Nietzsche, *The Gay Science*, trans. Walter Kaufmann (New York: Vintage Books, 1974), 181-182.

4. Prayer adapted from C. Frederick Barbee and Paul F. M. Zahl, *The Collects of Thomas Cranmer* (Grand Rapids: Eerdmans, 1999), 50.

SESSION 4

1. Roger L. Hahn, *Matthew: A Commentary for Bible Students* (Indianapolis: Wesleyan Publishing House, 2007), 239-240.

SESSION 5

1. Frederick Buechner, *Whistling in the Dark: A Doubter's Dictionary* (San Francisco: HarperSanFrancisco, 1988), 36-37.

2. Francis A. Schaeffer, *The Mark of the Christian* (Downers Grove: InterVarsity Press, 1970), 34; available at Calvin College Ethereal Library (www.ccel.us/schaeffer.html), accessed September 21, 2010.

SESSION 6

1. Gordon Fee and Douglas Stuart, *How to Read the Bible for All Its Worth* (Grand Rapids: Zondervan, 2003), 22.

2. Willaim Klein, Craig Blomberg, and Robert Hubbard, *Introduction to Biblical Interpretation* (Nashville: W Publishing, 1993), 425.

GOOD QUESTION BIBLE STUDIES SERIES CONTRIBUTORS

• ARTICLE AUTHORS •

D. A. Carson is research professor of New Testament at Trinity Evangelical Divinity School.

Timothy George is dean of Beeson Divinity School of Samford University and an executive editor of *Christianity Today*.

Stanley J. Grenz was professor of theology at Carey/Regent College in Vancouver, British Columbia, Canada, and at Northern Baptist Theological Seminary in Illinois.

Christopher A. Hall is professor of biblical and theological studies at Eastern University in St. Davids, Pennsylvania, and a *Christianity Today* editor-at-large.

Craig S. Keener is a visiting professor at Eastern Seminary in Philadelphia and author of *The IVP Bible Background Commentary: New Testament*.

R. Todd Mangum is Professor of Theology and Dean of the Faculty at Biblical Seminary in Hatfield, Pennsylvania.

Alister McGrath is Professor of Theology, Ministry and Education, and Head of the Center for Theology, Religion, and Culture at King's College, London. He is the author of many books, including *Mere Theology* and *The Dawkins Delusion?*

Roger E. Olson is professor of theology at George W. Truett Theological Seminary of Baylor University and author of *The Westminster Handbook to Evangelical Theology*.

Nancy Ortberg is a church leadership consultant and popular speaker. Formerly a teaching pastor at Willow Creek Community Church in Illinois, she now lives in California with her husband, John.

J. I. Packer is Board of Governors' Professor of Theology at Regent College and a member of the editorial council for *Christianity Today*.

Arthur O. Roberts is professor-at-large at George Fox University and author of *Exploring Heaven: What Great Christian Thinkers Tell Us About Our Afterlife with God* (HarperSan-Francisco).

Bruce Shelley was church history professor at Denver Seminary.

Lewis B. Smedes was professor emeritus of theology and ethics at Fuller Theological Seminary and author of *The Art of Forgiving: When You Need to Forgive and Don't Know How*.

Allen Verhey is a professor of Christian Ethics at Duke Divinity School.

• BIBLE STUDY AUTHORS •

Tracey Bianchi is the Pastor for Women at Christ Church of Oak Brook and is an activist, writer, and speaker on Christians and the environment. She earned her MDiv from Denver Seminary. You can visit her at traceybianchi.com.

Christopher Blumhofer is an ordination candidate in the Presbyterian church. His writings have appeared in *Leadership* journal, *Relevant*, and BuildingChurchLeaders.com.

Amie Hollman is a freelance writer, graphic designer, and illustrator who has contributed work for *Radiant, Sojourners, Neue* online, *Light & Life*, and the *LIVE Bible (NLT)*. She lives with her family in New York City, where her husband is a pastor at a multicultural church in Queens.

Jan Johnson is the author of twenty books, including *Invitation to the Jesus Life,* and many magazine articles and Bible studies. Also a speaker and spiritual director, she holds a DMin in Ignatian spirituality (www.JanJohnson.org).

Joy-Elizabeth Lawrence is a writer, actor, coauthor of Grand Days, and a staff member at Calvin College. You can find her at www.joyelizabethlawrence.wordpress.com.

Michael Mack is the Life Groups Minister at Northeast Christian Church in Louisville, Kentucky. He is founder of SmallGroups.com and SmallGroupLeadership.com, and has written numerous books about small group leadership, including *I'm a Leader . . . Now What?* (Standard Publishing).

Kevin Miller served for many years as Vice President at Christianity Today International. He recently left CTI to pursue full-time ministry as a pastor in the Chicago area.

Jason and Alison Tarka are writers and musicians. They pastor and minister together in an urban church in Portland, Oregon.

David Trujillo is a Bible teacher, adult ministry leader, and a columnist for *GROUP* magazine.

Kelli B. Trujillo is an adult ministry leader and the author of several books, including *Faith-Filled Moments* (Wesleyan).

Kyle White is the founding director of Neighbors' House, an outreach to at-risk students in DeKalb County, Illinois. He is a freelance writer, frequent contributor to Christian BibleStudies.com, and author of *Wisconsin River of Grace*. Kyle can be found at KyleLWhite .blogspot.com.

Heather Gemmen Wilson is a best-selling author and an award-winning international speaker. She is married to a pastor, and together they have six children.

ADDITIONAL BOOKS IN THE GOOD QUESTION SERIES

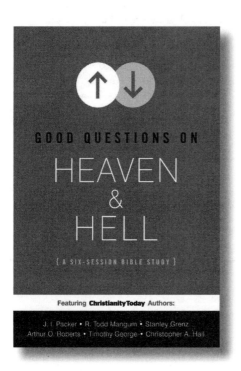

Good Questions on Heaven & Hell
Considering these questions:
- Where is Heaven and how will we experience it?
- Why would a loving God punish people with eternal torture?
- What do we gain from bodily resurrection?
Item #021556510

Good Questions on Right & Wrong
Considering these questions:
- Can lying ever be justified?
- Are all sins equal?
- Should Christians take care of the earth?
Item # 021556610

Visit your local Christian bookstore or www.standardpub.com